CW00346169

Regional Steam

Around Britain in the 1950s

by Brian Morrison

Published by
Railway Herald

ABOVE: *With Caley 2F 0-6-0 No. 57253 coming off shed on the left, Peppercorn Class A2 Pacific No. 60531 'Bahram' shrouds Aberdeen Ferryhill in thick smoke on 25th June 1957, with the 17.17 express from Aberdeen to Edinburgh Waverley.*

Front Cover:
Climbing away from Copenhagen Tunnel on 11th July 1953, Gresley 'A4' No. 60003 'Andrew K. McCosh' heads north from King;s Cross with the 09.40 'Norwegian Express' for Newcastle Tyne Commission Quay.

Front Cover (Bottom Left):
Stanier 5MT Mogul No. 42929 of Brunswich (8E) shed awaits departure from Liverpool Central station on 22nd August 1955, with the 11.43 local service to Stockport.

Front Cover (Bottom Middle):
Standing beneath Sir John Hawkshaw's great crescent roof at Cannon Street station before it was torn down in April 1958, allegedly because it was unsafe due to wartime bomb damage, West Country Pacific No. 34100 'Appledore' is at the head of an evening Ramsgate train on 25th April 1952.

Front Cover (Bottom Right):
The 'Cambrian Coast Express' from Paddington to Aberystwyth, with through coaches for Barmouth and Pwllheli, passes Wellington signalbox and approaches the station on 30th August 1952, powered by 7800 class 'Manor' 4-6-0 No. 7818 'Granville Manor'.

Frontispeace:
Gresley V2 class 2-6-2 No. 60889 passes Holgate sidings on 22nd May 1959, taking the line to Skelton Junction to avoid passing through York station. The train consists of planked design 12-ton ventilated vans.

Rear Cover:
The 09.50 express from Aberdeen arrives at Edinburgh Waverley on 31st July 1953 behind Class A2 Pacific No. 60529 'Pearl Diver', which took over the train at Dundee. This was the only locomotive in the A2 fleet to have been rebuilt with a double blast pipe and multiple valve regulator.

First published 2009

ISBN 978-0-9562581-0-6

All rights reserved. No part of this book may be reproduced or transmitted, in any form or by any means, electronic or mechanical, including photocopying, recording or by an information storage and retrieval system, without permission from the Publisher in writing.

© Brian Morrison / Railway Herald 2009
Maps © Sim Harris 2009

Published by Railway Herald Limited,
PO Box 252, Scunthorpe, North Lincolnshire.
DN17 2WY
Telephone: 01904 500175.
E-Mail: info@rhpublishing.co.uk

Printed in England by Ian Allan Printing Limited,
Hersham, Surrey. KT12 4RG

Details on all titles published by Railway Herald can be found on our website, available 24 hours a day, at:
http://www.rhpublishing.co.uk

Contents

BELOW: *In the very untidy yard next to the coaling stage at Sheffield (Grimesthorpe) shed (19A) on 27th August 1955, sit Midland 2F 0-6-0 No. 58225 and 3F 0-6-0 No. 43388, ready for their next duty.*

Introduction

Having been a railway enthusiast from schooldays (or an 'engine spotter' as we were then known), I would like to have started railway photography in the late 1940s before many of the locomotives retained for use during the war years were scrapped – but instead I had to endure two-and-a-half –years of Army National Service.

On demob in 1951, I spent most of my gratuity on an Agfa Isolette 6cm x 6cm camera, selected because it had a top shutter speed of 1/500th of a second to enable me to 'stop' moving trains. Using the top shutter speed quite extensively, the spring mechanism became less efficient over the years and the 1/500th became nearer to a 1/200th. An Agfa Isolette II was obtained with an excellent f3.5 Solinar lens, but with a top shutter speed of 1/300th my lineside activities became restricted to stations, engine sheds and slow-moving lines. Emulating the top railway photographers of the day, such as Eric Treacy, Maurice Early, Ernest Wethersett, Jack Flemons and the like, I supplemented the Isolette II with a quarter-plate reflex. The second-hand Thornton Pickard camera was very much larger and heavier than the 6cm x 6cm, but boasted a f3.5 Tessar lens and a 1/1000th of a second top shutter speed.

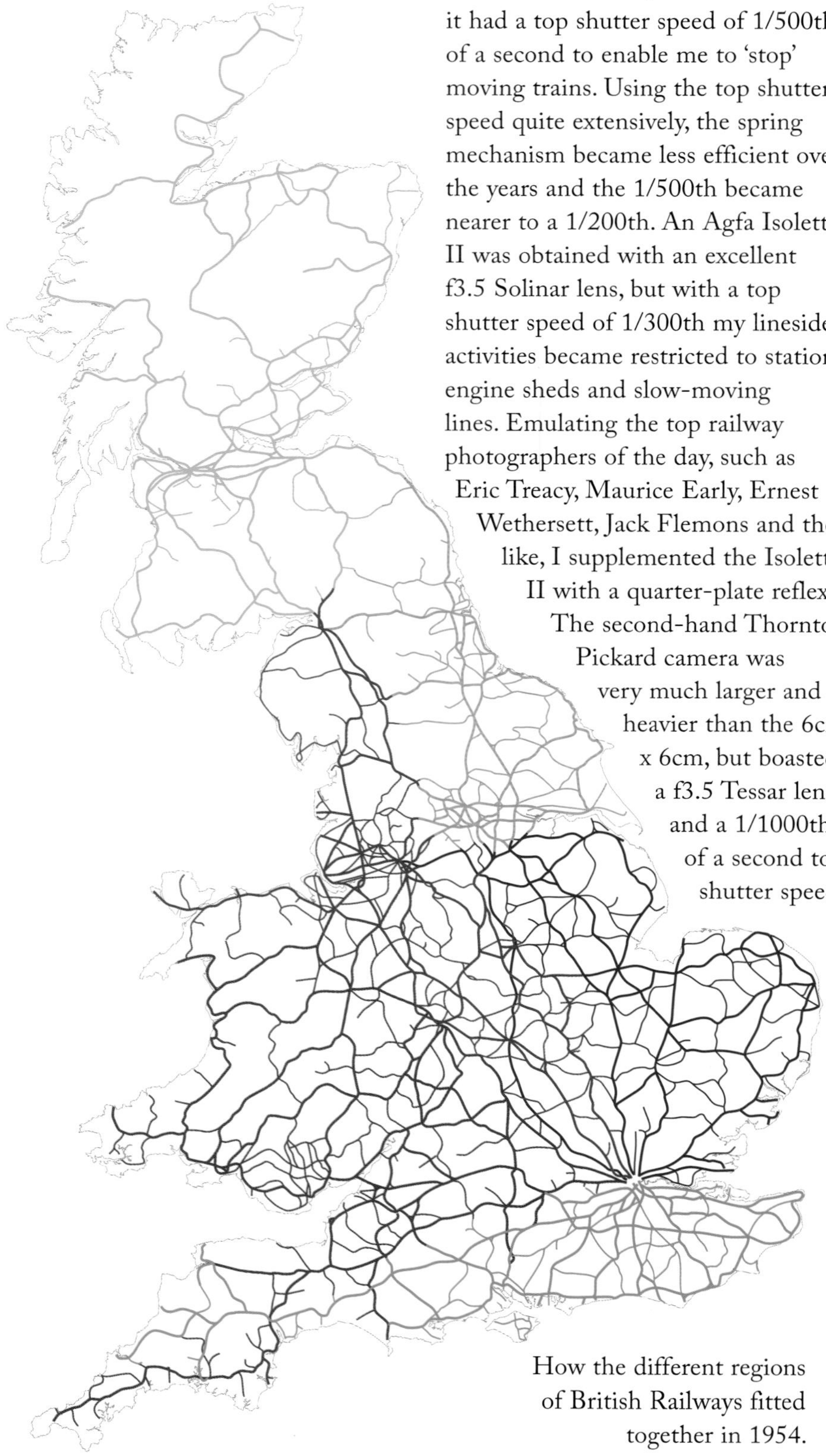

How the different regions of British Railways fitted together in 1954.

To avoid using glass plates, I had fitted a 9cm x 6cm roll-film holder, and when the focal plane shutter decided it would work properly (about 50% of the time), I obtained some of my best-ever results at lineside, but also lost many. Both cameras were eventually traded in for a Rollieflex and in later years I graduated to a Bronica and then to a series of Nikons.

Not being able to afford a car in the early days, most of my initial activities were in south-east London on a bicycle or local visits to the other Regions by train. After having a number of photographs published in the Railway Magazine and Trains Illustrated, I started to apply for lineside photographic permits, which were then issued by the Regions in order to obtain free publicity for their services by means of published magazine illustrations. The Southern was not keen on allowing access to third-rail areas, but apart from that, the permit was all-Regional. The Eastern and Midland Regions initially allowed a short stretch of lineside, which was increased upon request at each annual renewal. The Western was not at all generous, and after many attempts, I managed to obtain permission to photograph in Sonning Cutting! When obtaining my first car, I applied to North Eastern and Scottish Regions, and both responded with all-Region passes. Looking at some of my prints from those days, I wonder what Health & Safety today would have thought of some of the positions taken up between tracks, up signal gantries, from signalbox ledges and the like – and of course hi-visibility vests had not been invented!

Photography was synonymous with black & white for most of the decade, as when colour film came about it was very expensive and too 'slow' to record anything moving – which is the reason why this album lacks any colour reproductions. Roll-film had been unobtainable during the war years and was very slow to come on to the market after hostilities ceased. The films considered the best were Ilford HP3 and Kodak Super XX, and many photographic shops and chemists kept both 'under the counter' for special customers, which meant that often Ilford Selochrome (recording reds as blacks) or some rather grainy Gaevert Gevapan or Agfa Isopan ISS had to be used. Film development and printing was at first undertaken for me by my frequent lineside companion, Arthur Carpenter, but eventually an underground dugout at the end of my garden, constructed by my father before war broke out, was converted by him to a perfect darkroom with a workbench and shelves, and I commenced my own processing. Being a smoker in those days, my mother wondered how I managed to survive the atmosphere while down there for hours on end with the mixed fumes from the cigarettes and the photo chemicals! The prints, however, were obviously well 'fixed' as I still have some that were produced in those days that have not discoloured. Today, computer 'light rooms' for digital photographers have replaced most darkrooms, and everything is so much easier and quicker. If only digital photography had been invented in the 1950s, I would not need my 16 ledgers, laboriously detailing when, where and what I had caught on film or the card index system giving dates and locations.

Upon returning to photography after a break for most of the 1960s, I was approached in 1973 by Ian Allan Publishing to compile an album called London Steam in the Fifties. This was followed by a number of small volumes for publishers Bradford Barton, and other titles followed in the 'Power' series for Oxford Publishing Company and for Silver Link in the publisher's 'Past & Present' series. Until this book, I had authored or co-authored 39 different titles over the years, this one rounding out the total to 40. Co-authors have included good friends such as John Vaughan, Colin Marsden, Ken Brunt and the late Stanley Creer and Brian Beer. If I live long enough, I hope to compile at least one more book in 2011 on my 60 years at the lineside.

ABOVE: *Class B17/1 'Sandringham' 4-6-0 No. 61625 'Raby Castle' is serviced in the yard at a very smokey London Liverpool Street on 7th March 1951, my first photograph on the day I obtained my first camera.*

A slight problem with a Regional book such as this, that spans almost a decade, is the number of changes that took place to the regional boundaries within the period covered. Fortunately, the majority of these occurred between 1947 and 1949, just before the period covered by this book, but a few did take place in the 1950s, and for the purposes of clarification I have chosen 1954 as the key year in this respect. Hence, the maps kindly supplied by Sim Harris and used in the title are correct to the best of our knowledge for 1954, although it has to be said that regional boundaries were not well documented in the period.

All the photographs were taken by myself.

BELOW: *U1 class Mogul No. 31900 departs from Redhill on 25th June 1951, hauling a through service from Hastings to Birkenhead.*

Western Region

ABOVE: *3100 class 2-6-2T No. 3102 heads northwards from the yards north of Wolverhampton Low Level on 20th July 1954, hauling both steel-sided and wooden-sided mineral wagons. The five locos that made up the class were 1938 Collett rebuilds of Churchwards 1906 '3150s' with higher boiler pressure and smaller wheels.*

Although my travels on the Western Region of the time did range from London to north and south Wales and to the West Country and Birkenhead, opportunities for lineside photography were not as plentiful as with the other five Regions, as the Public Relations office was extremely reluctant to issue such passes.

Frequent opportunities were presented at Shrewsbury, however, as a relation was a signalman there! Staff at Oswestry were always friendly, and Wellington was easy, as another relation's house had the mainline at the end of her garden – and the fence was not very high! I was also able to record much of the variety of motive power that presented itself at Swindon Works, either for overhaul or for scrapping. This was thanks to the group visits ably organised by the Railway Correspondence & Travel Society.

As with all my photography in the 1950s, my interest lay more with obtaining all the different locomotive varieties that were still in traffic, rather than visiting locations where I did not expect to see anything that I had not already recorded. As a result some parts of the system were omitted from my travels, all journeys for the majority of the decade being by train, as I did not manage to obtain my first car until 1958.

In terms of the motive power on the Western, I managed to obtain a photograph of all 50 types that were available before being scrapped, with the exception of a few examples taken on by the GWR from the Rhymney and Swansea Harbour Trust Railways, where the cutters torches got to them before I did!

It is quite remarkable that the works at Swindon remained almost geographically in the centre of the Western Region network throughout its life, even after the addition of other routes such as the Cambrian.

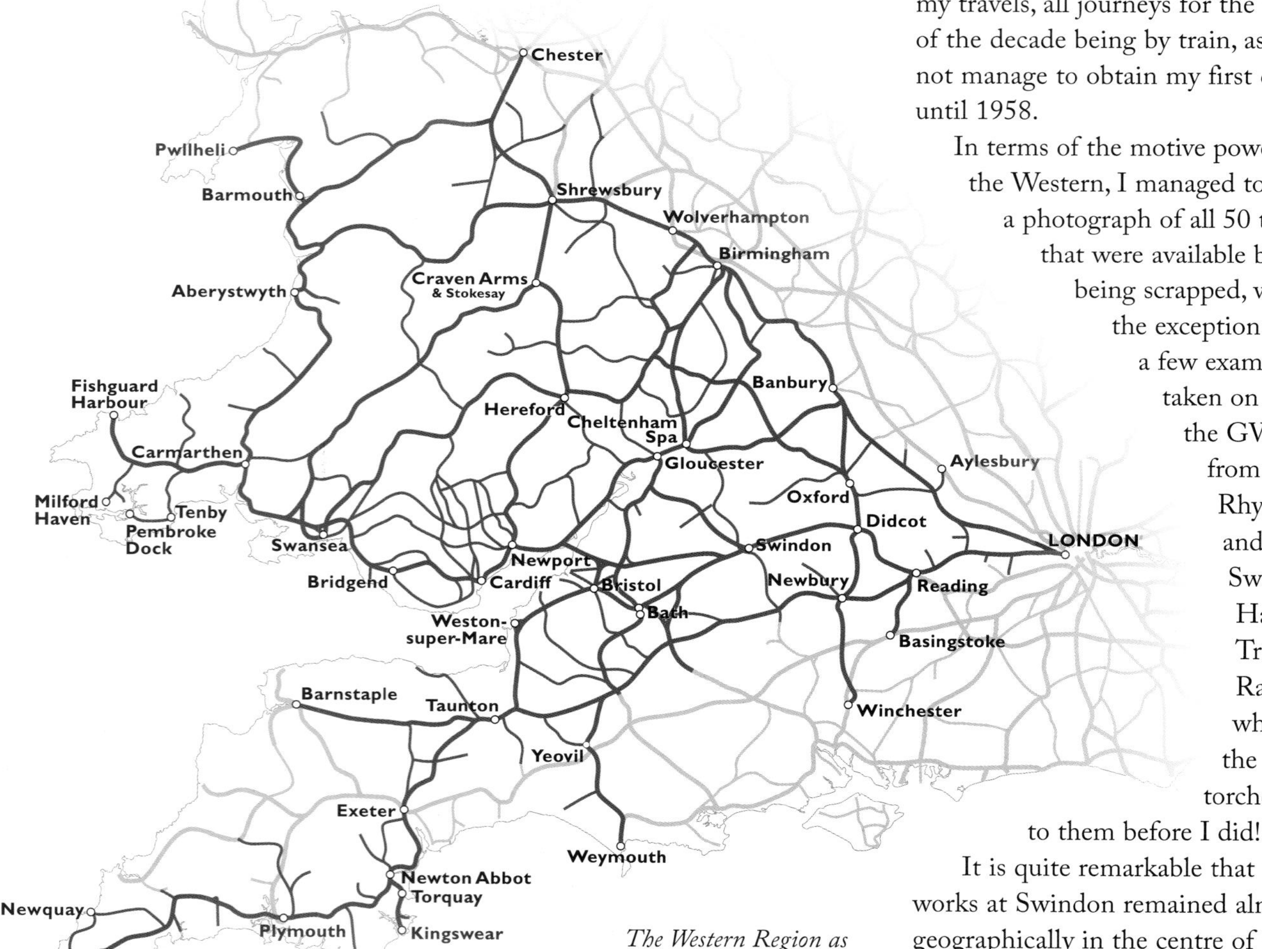

The Western Region as it was around 1954. The likes of, what are now, the Gloucestershire Warwickshire Railway and the South Devon Railway can clearly be seen.

ABOVE: *At the head of the 18.55 express to Swansea, BR Standard 7MT 'Britannia' Pacific No. 70020 'Mercury' awaits departure time at London Paddington on 6th November 1952, before heading out into the night.*

BELOW: *The 11.55 express to Pembroke Dock departs from Paddington on 3rd August 1958, and passes under Ranelagh Bridge, fronted by 'Hall' 4-6-0 No. 4991 'Cobham Hall'. To the Great Western, the 'Hall' class locomotives were the equivilent to the LMS 'Black 5s', being almost go-anywhere locomotives that were equally at home on either passenger or freight duties.*

ABOVE: *An express from Bristol Temple Meads to London Paddington passes Southall at speed on 5th May 1956, powered by 'Castle' class 4-6-0 No. 5029 'Nunney Castle'.*

LEFT: *At Ruscombe, near Twyford, on 8th July 1951, 'King' class 4-6-0 No. 6007 'King William III' provides the unexpected sight of a top link express locomotive on a westbound rake of milk tank empties, albeit quite a fast one!*

BELOW: *On 15th February 1952, the funeral train of King George VI passes Iver, ostensibly headed by 'Castle' class 4-6-0 No. 4082 'Windsor Castle'. In fact, the 'Royal Engine' was undergoing overhaul at Swindon at this time and No. 7013 'Bristol Castle' was suitably 'disguised' for the occasion. The resplendent locomotive displays the Royal Crest on both sides and carries four headlamps, the top one surmounted by a crown.*

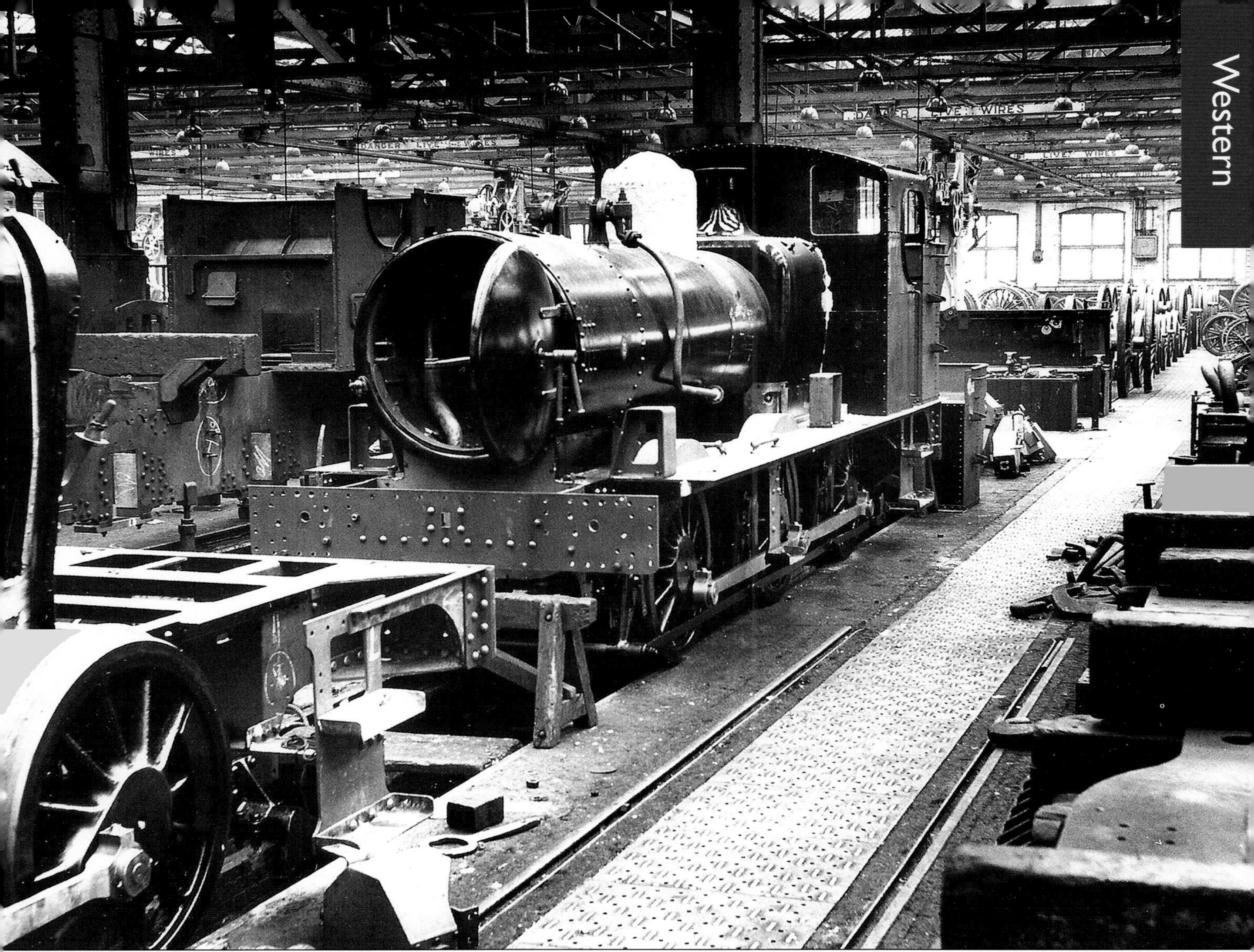

ABOVE: *Swindon Works was a mecca for enthusiasts, especially when in the 1950s, visits were possible. For the Great Western Railway and later British Railways Western Region, the workshops were a 'key' part of railway operations, building and maintaining a large number of steam locomotives to both Great Western and British Railways designs, and in later years diesels as well. On 13th February 1955, a Class 1600 0-6-0PT No. 1660 is under construction in the Erecting Shop.*

RIGHT: *While undergoing its seemingly interminable testing for poor steaming in its British Railways days, Class 8P Pacific No. 71000 'Duke of Gloucester' looks out from the Swindon workshop known as the 'Barn' on the same day. Only three of the various variety of chimneys in the foreground has a capuchon, which is the raised lip at the front of a chimney, intended to prevent down draughts when in motion. Part of its role was intended to help in lifting smoke away from the crew's line of sight.*

2883
WAITING AND
LADIES ROOMS

ABOVE: *The 10.35 Paignton-Wolverhampton cross-country express approaches Stratford-upon-Avon on 15th August 1958, headed by 'Hall' class 4-6-0 No. 4980 'Wrottesley Hall'. Class 5100 2-6-2T No. 5163 is looped with a freight awaiting its passing.*

PREVIOUS PAGE: *2800 class 2-8-0 No. 2883 passes through Stratford-upon-Avon station on the following day, hauling a freight working to Severn Tunnel Junction.*

BELOW: *Hawksworth 'County' 4-6-0 No. 1025 'County of Radnor' approaches Stratford-upon-Avon on 16th August 1958, with empty coaching stock to form a return excursion to Manchester London Road.*

ABOVE: *Waiting to depart from Birmingham Snow Hill on 16th August 1958, 'Manor' class 4-6-0 No. 7821 'Ditcheat Manor' heads the 11.00 train for Pwllheli. This locomotive was one of several 'Manor' class engines that, thanks to Barry Scrapyard, escaped the cutters' torch and now operate on heritage lines.*

BELOW: *Approaching Wellington ten days earlier, on 6th August 1956, 'Castle' class 4-6-0 No. 7010 'Avondale Castle' heads the 'Cambrian Coast Express' from Aberystwyth to London Paddington.*

ABOVE: *Originally a Robinson-design for the Great Central (becoming LNER Class O4) the same design of locomotives were built from 1917 onwards for the Railway Operating Division and taken on by the GWR. The class were always known as the ROD 2-8-0s. On 30th August 1952, No. 3031 clearly shows its non-GWR lines as it heads through Wellington, in Shropshire, with a mixed freight for Oxley.*

LEFT: *The 'Cambrian Coast Express' from London Paddington to Aberystwyth, with through coaches for Barmouth and Pwllheli, passes Wellington signalbox and approaches the station on 30th August 1952, powered by 7800 class 'Manor' 4-6-0 No. 7818 'Granville Manor'. The 'Cambrian Coast Express' first operated in 1927 on Fridays and Saturdays only, and originally avoided Shrewsbury, the locomotive change taking place at Wolverhampton. When the Shrewsbury stop was introduced, the engine change took place there instead. After a period of being just a 'Saturdays only' service, the train became daily from 1954.*

ABOVE: *At Shrewsbury on 28th August 1952, 'Hall' class 4-6-0 No. 4976 'Warfield Hall' departs with all Southern-green coaching stock, forming a Hastings to Birkenhead inter-regional express, while Class 8F 2-8-0 No. 48706 is signal-checked in the centre road with a freight for Crewe, and in the shadow of the station canopy on the right, is 'Saint' 4-6-0 No. 2933 'Bibury Court, awaiting departure with the 16.50 local service for Gobowen.*

BELOW: *An express working for Barmouth leaves Ruabon on 9th August 1956, hauled by 4300 class Mogul No. 7310 piloting 2251 class 0-6-0 No. 2209.*

CATCH POINTS IN
DOWN MAIN LINE
650 YARDS

VIROL
9013

LEFT: *Departing from Welshpool on 13th August 1958, 2251 class 0-6-0 No. 2274 heads the 09.55 local service from Oswestry to Shrewsbury.*

BELOW LEFT: *Ex-GWR 'Dukedog' 4-4-0 No. 9013 awaits departure from Welshpool on 10th August 1956 with the 17.20 service to Shrewsbury. Only one member of the 'Dukedog' class made it into preservation, that being No. 9017 'Earl of Berkeley', built at Swindon Works in 1938 and preserved in 1962. The locomotive is in working order and is based on the Bluebell Railway.*

BELOW: *One of the locos based at Oswestry (89A) at this time, Ivatt 2MT Mogul No. 46523 arrives at Llanymynech with the 13.28 train from Oswestry to Welshpool. The station sign reads 'Change for Llanfyllin Branch and Lake Vyrnwy'. Both Llanymynech and Llanfyllin stations were closed in 1965 – but Lake Vyrnwy is still there, providing you have a car or travel by bus!*

ABOVE: *On a wet 14th August 1958 at Aberystwyth, the 09.55 semi-fast train to Shrewsbury awaits departure time with 4300 class Mogul No. 6378 of Machynlleth shed (89C) providing the traction.*

LEFT: *Ex-Rhymney Railway R1 class 0-6-2T No. 36 outside its home depot of Cardiff East Dock (88B) on 21st July 1957.*

BELOW: *With two local residents looking rather bemused at someone photographing their train in the pouring rain, Class 4500 2-6-2T No. 4560 arrives at Dovey Junction on 4th August 1958 with the 09.30 train from Barmouth to Machynlleth.*

ABOVE: *In ex-works condition, 7200 class 2-8-2T No. 7217 stands inside Cardiff Canton shed on 21st July 1957, alongside work-stained 4200 class 2-8-0T No. 4207. The '4200' was a resident of Canton (86C), but the '7200' was allocated to Swansea Landore (87E) at this time.*

BELOW: *Jones-designed 1903 Cambrian Railways '89' class 0-6-0 No. 895 arrives at Oswestry on 22nd July 1954, with the 13.25 local service from Gobowen.*

LEFT: *The 2ft 6in gauge Welshpool & Llanfair Railway 0-6-0T No. 822 (previously 'The Earl'), built by Beyer Peacock in Gorton, Manchester, in 1903, approaches Ravens Square, Welshpool, on 10th August 1956 with a freight working.*

BELOW: *After closure of the Welshpool & Llanfair Railway (W&LR) in 1956, its two Beyer Peacock 1902-built 0-6-0Ts Nos. 822 and 823 were stored under cover inside Oswestry Works, hopefully awaiting preservation, where they were recorded here on 14th August 1958. Now in steam on the preserved eight-mile W&LR line, they have been returned to their original numbers 1 and 2 and names 'The Earl' and 'The Countess'.*

ABOVE: *Hauling the 11.50 Taunton-Castle Cary local service on 12th May 1958, bunker-first 4575 class 2-6-2T No. 5554 sets out from Taunton on its short journey.*

BELOW: *With vans for Bristol, 'Grange' class 4-6-0 No. 6835 'Eastham Grange' approaches Taunton on the same day.*

ABOVE: *'The Royal Duchy' from Paddington to Penzance arrives at Newton Abbot on 10th May 1958, powered by 4073 'Castle' class 4-6-0 No. 7027 'Thornbury Castle', one of the Old Oak Common (81A) allocation.*

BELOW: *Later the same day, 'Castle' class 4-6-0 No. 5075 'Wellington' approaches Bodmin Road station with the 'The Cornishman' express from Penzance to Wolverhampton Low Level.*

ABOVE: *Ex-works 4900 class 'Hall' 4-6-0 No. 5907 'Marble Hall' passes the photographer near Denham on 11th April 1953, hauling a westbound mixed freight.*

OVERLEAF: *In the days when Paddington-Birkenhead expresses travelled via the Chilterns, blue-liveried 'King' 4-6-0 No. 6016 'King Edward V' passes near Seer Green with the 16.10 from London.*

BELOW: *Also on 11th April 1953, ex-War Department 2-8-0 No. 90207 passes near Denham hauling a lengthy eastbound mixed freight. With their familiar clanking noise, the 'Dub-Dees' could easily be heard approaching!*

ABOVE: *Allocated to Gloucester (85A), Collett Class 2251 0-6-0 No. 2290 passes Denham West Junction signalbox on 11th April 1953 and crosses the Grand Union Canal, south of Denham, with a freight for Neasden yard.*

BELOW: *Ivatt 2MT 2-6-2T No. 41243 is about to depart from Bath Green Park on 21st April 1956 with the 12.23 local service to Bristol Temple Meads.*

ABOVE: *6100 class Prairie tank No. 6103 approaches High Wycombe with a local service from Banbury on 6th June 1953.*

Southern Region

ABOVE: *A RCTS special over little-used lines in East Sussex on 4th October 1953, waits to leave Three Bridges on its travels behind an immaculately prepared 'last in class' D3 0-4-4T No. 32390.*

Living in Kent on the outskirts of London, the mainlines from Charing Cross, Victoria and Cannon Street were within cycling distance, and there was little reason to travel to the extremities of the county as practically all motive power that visited the Kent Coast passed me at Chislehurst or Bickley!

Nevertheless, with an all-Region lineside pass (excluding third-rail areas) I did pay visits to Hildenborough, Westerham, Tonbridge, Ashford and Dover for various reasons, and of course the Region also stretched westwards from Waterloo to the West Country, where photographs were obtained at the likes of Eastleigh, Exeter, Axminster/Lyme Regis and Wadebridge.

The south coast of the Western Section of the Southern could not be ignored, and the Isle of Wight engines were first obtained on film while I was there on honeymoon in 1952! Also, there was the likes of Brighton and the Somerset & Dorset that had to be included.

Locations that I now wish I had managed to visit in those days include those on the west coast of Cornwall, as well as Portsmouth and Plymouth. As regards the number of locomotive classes and sub-classes in traffic on Southern metals, there was over 60 at work on the distinctly different Eastern, Central and Western Sections, which today are the separate franchises for Southeastern, Southern and South West Trains; even the West Country Pacifics, when the class was increased for use on the Eastern Section, were classified as Battle of Britain Pacifics, as it was not thought appropriate that locos with West Country town names should be seen in Kent! The occasional Battle of Britain did manage to stray onto the Western Section but I never saw a West Country on the Eastern Section!

By the end of the decade, I had managed to obtain a photographic record of all the types, and this required travelling to Wadebridge for the Beattie Well Tanks, to Hayling Island for the Class A1X 'Terriers' and to Lyme Regis for the Adams 0415 class 'Radials'.

ABOVE: *At Waterloo on Leap Year Day 1952, ex-SE&CR D class 4-4-0 No. 31746 was unexpected motive power for the 20.13 parcels train to Reading.*

OVERLEAF: *'The Cunarder' was a prestigious Pullman boat train bringing Cunard White Star voyagers from abroad back to London Waterloo from Southanpton Docks. On 25th July 1956, the train nears the end of it journey and passes through Clapham Junction, hauled by 'Lord Nelson' 4-6-0 No. 30860 'Lord Hawke'.*

BELOW: *Between 4COR electric unit No. 3149, forming a train to Portsmouth Harbour, and H16 class Pacific Tank No. 30520 with empty coaching stock, Maunsell 'King Arthur' 4-6-0 No. 30751 'Etarre' departs from Waterloo on 23rd August 1952, with a train for Bournemouth West.*

CUNARDER
SPL
4

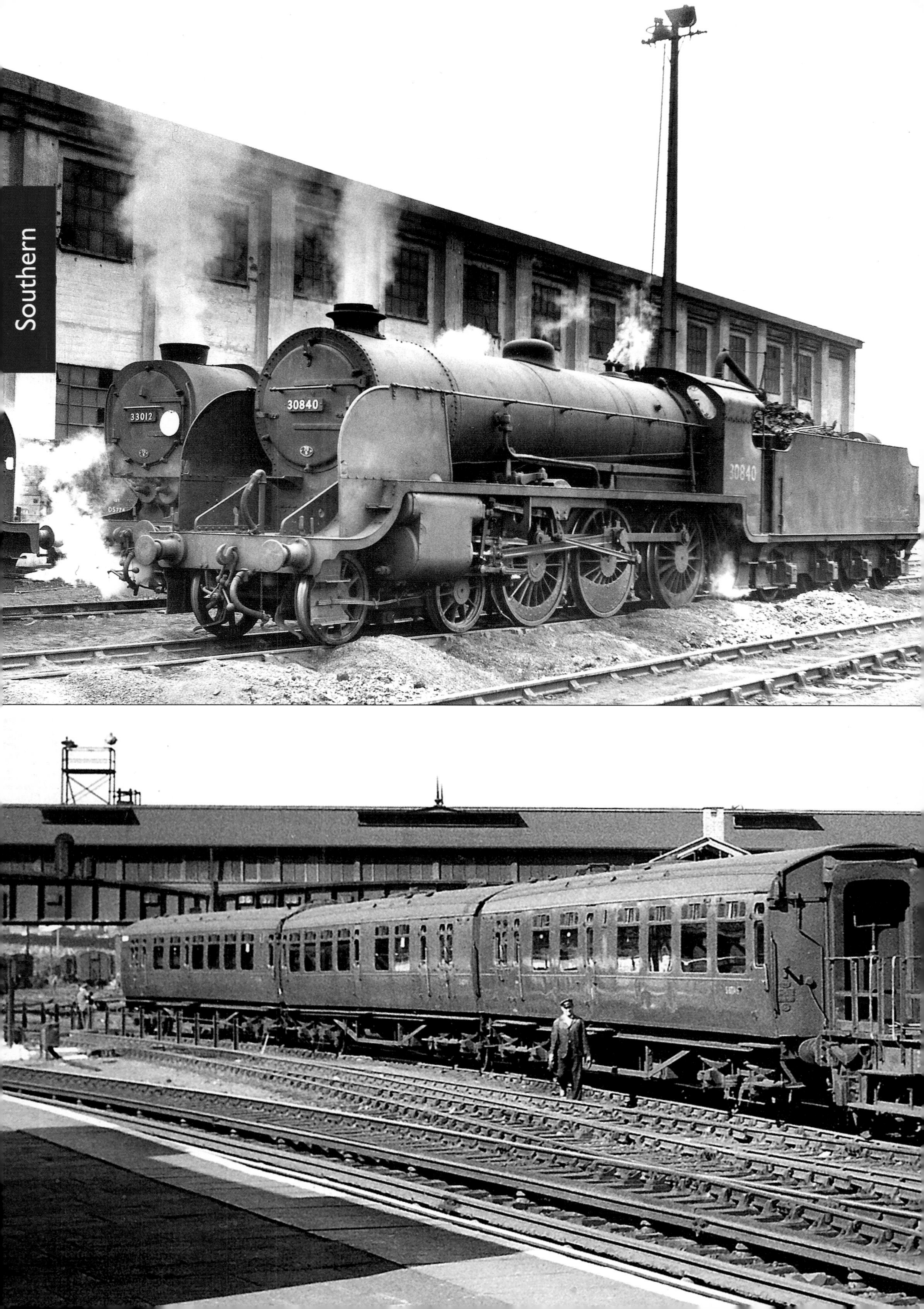
33012
30840
30840

ABOVE: *The last of the L&SWR Drummond S11 class 4-4-0s No. 30400 under the coaling plant at Guildford (70C) shed on 1st September 1951, three years before it was finally condemned.*

LEFT: *Outside Feltham shed (70B) on a dull and misty 21st May 1955, Maunsell Class S15 4-6-0 No. 30840 and Bulleid Class Q1 0-6-0 No. 33012 are both residents, and both are coaled and watered ready to depart for their next respective duties.*

BELOW: *A Billinton design for the LB&SCR introduced in 1910, Class E4 0-6-2T No. 32476 marshalls coaches in Clapham yard on 25th July 1956. The shunters truck attached was converted from an old Beattie tender.*

ABOVE: *A1X class 'Terrier' 0-6-0T No. 32661 hauls a train for Hayling Island away from Alton on 1st September 1951.*

BELOW: *Crossing the rail viaduct over the Langstone Channel to Hayling Island, the branch train from Havant is headed by Class A1X 'Terrier' 0-6-0T No. 32655, the same day.*

ABOVE: *Hauling a Plymouth to Nine Elms mixed freight, Urie L&SWR H15 class 4-6-0 No. 30487 rounds the curve under Battledown Viaduct, west of Basingstoke, on 8th September 1952.*

BELOW: *A 1907 Hawthorn Leslie design for the Plymouth Devonport & South Western Junction Railway, Class 757 0-6-2T No. 30758 'Lord St Levan' is in a line-up of unwanted locomotives at Eastleigh Works on 25th July 1956.*

ABOVE: *Bristol Bath Road (82A)-allocated 'Hall' 4-6-0 No. 5919 'Worsley Hall' on Southern metals at Salisbury on 2nd July 1954, restarts a cross-country express travelling from Southampton to Cardiff General.*

BELOW: *Acting as Exeter Central station pilot on 11th May 1958, BR Standard 3MT 2-6-2T No. 82024 engages in shunting duties..*

ABOVE: *One of the four E1 0-6-0Ts allocated to the Isle of Wight for non-passanger duties, No. 2 'Yarmouth' undergoes bogie repairs out in the open at Newport shed/works yard (71E) on 24th June 1953.*

BELOW: *One of only two Isle of Wight 02 class 0-4-4Ts fitted with push-pull apparatus, No. 36 'Carisbrooke' stands at Freshwater on 26th June 1953 with the 14.00 service to Newport.*

31831

ABOVE: *Much rebuilt Beattie L&SWR Class 0298 2-4-0 Well Tank No. 30586 shunts at Wadebridge on 10th May 1958. Of note is the line up of hand carts on the left-hand side of the picture. The station was closed in 1967.*

PREVIOUS PAGE: *N class Mogul No. 31831 emerges from Blackboy tunnel, near Exeter, on 11th May 1958, hauling a Sunday engineers' train.*

BELOW: *Allocated to the Southern shed of Plymouth (72D), Class 02 0-4-4T No. 30236 departs from Wadebridge on 10th May 1958 with the 09.48 local service to Bodmin North. The '02s' were an 1889 Adams design for the L&SWR.*

ABOVE: *Standing beneath Sir John Hawkshaw's great crescent roof at Cannon Street station before it was torn down in April 1958, allegedly because it was unsafe due to wartime bomb damage, West Country Pacific No. 34100 'Appledore' is at the head of an evening Ramsgate train on 25th April 1952.*

ABOVE: *Hauling 'birdcage' coaching stock, Marsh LB&SCR Class H2 Atlantic No. 32426 'St Albans Head' departs from London Bridge terminus on 25th June 1952, hauling the 17.40 train to Newhaven, a regular working for these locos at the time.*

BELOW: *A train of vans from Dover coasts into London Bridge in the late evening of 7th July 1953, hauled by Ashford (74A)-allocated Wainwright SE&CR C class 0-6-0 No. 31513.*

ABOVE: *A Kent Coast express from Cannon Street to Folkestone and Dover passes through London Bridge on 5th April 1952, powered by Battle of Britain Pacific No. 34078 '222 Squadron', which is still carrying original livery.*

BELOW: *A locomotive that still passes this way today, Battle of Britain Pacific No. 34067 'Tangmere', climbs the incline between Bickley and Bickley Junction on 27th July 1955, powering the 'Kentish Belle' Pullman from London Victoria to Margate and Ramsgate. Note the tall semaphore signals, almost covered by the light haze from the chimney, allowing drivers to see a clear sight of the signal as they approach the bridge.*

GOLDEN
ARROW

LEFT: *With a vans train bound for Bricklayets Arms passing above on the St Mary Cray-Chislehurst loop line, 'King Arthur' 4-6-0 No. 30791 'Sir Uwaine' passes between Bickley and St Mary Cray Junctions on 26th January 1952, hauling an express from London Victoria to Ramsgate.*

BELOW LEFT: *Coming off the main line and taking the Bickley-Petts Wood loop, the southbound 'Golden Arrow on 7th April 1954 is powered by Merchant Navy Pacific No. 35028 'Clan Line', in its days prior to being rebuilt without the streamline casing. This picture was quite well known in the 1950s as it was published as one of Valentines 'Real Train Photos' postcards.*

BELOW: *On the connecting loop line between St Mary Cray Junction and Chislehurst on a spring-like 20th February 1953, Maunsell SE&CR N class Mogul No. 31404 hauls loaded wooden-sided coal wagons from Betteshanger Colliery towards London.*

ABOVE: *On a clear and sunny 21st April 1951, Schools class 4-4-0 No. 30905 'Tonbridge' steams freely between Chislehurst and Petts Wood with an express working from Charing Cross to Hastings.*

BELOW: *Passing what can only be termed as a lineside garden shed, 'Schools' class 4-4-0 No. 30914 'Lancing' heads along the mainline towatds Petts Wood on 4th April 1954, bound for Tunbridge Wells Central and Hastings with an express from Cannon Street. The coaching stock is specially gauged to pass through BoPeep tunnel, Hastings.*

ABOVE: *Wainwright SE&CR Class H 0-4-4T No. 31239 approaches Dunton Green on 26th March 1953, with the 09.54 branch train from Westerham, a line closed in 1961.*

BELOW: *Departing from its only intermediate stop, the 12.58 service from Tonbridge to Sevenoaks begins the climb of Hildenborough bank on 23rd May 1953, the 'birdcage' coaching stock hauled by Kirtley LC&DR R class 0-4-4T No. 31666.*

ABOVE: *A passing of the ways on Hidenborough bank on 23rd May 1953. 'Britannia' Pacific No. 70009 'Alfred the Great' heads downgrade with a London Victoria-Folkestone Harbour boat train, while 'King Arthur' 4-6-0 No. 30769 'Sir Balan' slugs up the incline with a freight bound for Bricklayers Arms.*

BELOW: *Allocated to Dover shed (74C), Schools class 4-4-0 No. 30921 'Shrewsbury' climbs Hildenborough bank on 23rd May 1953 with an express from Dover Marine to London. When Bulleid fitted a multiple jet blastpipe and larger chimney to some half of the class in 1938, the performance of the locomotives certainly improved - but not their appearance!*

ABOVE: *Travelling at over 80mph, a down 'Continental Express' from London Victoria approaches Ashford on 22nd May 1954, powered by Bulleid Merchant Navy Pacific No. 35026 'Brocklebank Line'.*

RIGHT: *One of only a few remaining 1878-introduced Stirling South Eastern Railway O class 0-6-0s remaining in traffic at this time, No. 31064 was rebuilt with a domed boiler and a new cab by Wainwright in 1903 and reclassified O1. On 22nd May 1954, the venerable old machine takes water at Ashford (74A).*

BELOW: *Wainwright South Eastern & Chatham Railway C class 0-6-0 No. 31719 and Billinton London Brighton & South Coast Railway K class Mogul No. 32347 undergo heavy overhaul in Ashford Works on 22nd May 1954.*

ABOVE: *A London Victoria-Hastings train, via the Mid-Kent line and Tonbridge, awaits departure from Ashford on 24th September 1955, headed by three-cylinder N1 class Hither Green (73C)-based Mogul No. 31822.*

BELOW: *Bricklayers Arms (73B)-allocated 'Schools' class 4-4-0 No. 30938 'St Olaves' emerges from Priory tunnel and prepares to stop at Dover Priory on 24th September 1955, on its first leg to Charing Cross with a special relief from Dover Marine.*

ABOVE: *In what was called Stroudley green, but was really yellow, the Brighton Works shunter, Class A1X 'Terrier' 0-6-0T No. 377S 'Brighton Works' stands outside the complex on 2nd October 1954.*

BELOW: *Inside a decidedly untidy Brighton Works on 2nd October 1954, H2 class Brighton Atlantic No. 32421 'South Foreland' receives a heavy overhaul.*

ABOVE: *The little-loved but much photographed Somerset & Dorset Joint line is the subject of our last views of the Southern Region. Approaching Bath Green Park on 21st April 1956, S&DJR 7F 2-8-0 No. 53805 hauls the 09.05 freight from Evercreech Junction to Bath.*

BELOW: *Taken from high up on the embankment, the southbound 'Pines Express' approaches Templecombe on the same day, powered by BR Standard 5MT 4-6-0 No. 73047.*

Midland Region

Stretching from London to Holyhead and Carlisle, and including the likes of Birmingham, Crewe, Derby, Liverpool and Manchester, this Region was diverse and interesting but difficult to cover in all aspects.

The London termini were easy for me to reach, and so were some excellent locations within their close proximity, such as Camden Bank, Bushey and Elstree, that were visited on more than one occasion. The likes of Stafford, Crewe, Liverpool, Manchester and Carlisle were travelled to by train, and I also managed to go to Wigan, Warrington, Derby and Blackburn to obtain examples of motive power that I had yet to record, but in the time available had to forego many locations that I would like to have visited, particularly Rugby, the Cumbrian Coast and the Settle & Carlisle. Leeds and Pontefract are included in this section of the book for the sake of clarity, although strictly speaking from the definitions of the regional boundries at the time, both locations should be in North Eastern Region!

Because the LMS did not adopt individual class identification, but was content to label all its engines for power and use, the Midland Region inherited 10 different 3Fs, eight 2Ps, five 0Fs and five 2Fs for me to track down and record, as well as some 50 other varieties plus the Sentinels, Bayer-Garratts and the 'Lickey Banker'. With the sole exception of the latter, the task was eventually accomplished, having managed to sort out the designer and build dates and different wheel arrangements of the different types with the same classification.

For clarification, from an operational point of view, the Midland Region boundry was just to the east of Skipton on both the Ilkley and Aire Valley Routes and to the north-east of Sheffield on what we know today as the main Cross-Country route.

The Great Central Route via Rugby, Leicester and Nottingham (part of which forms today's Great Central Railway) came under Midland Region control during the period of this book, but only towards the very end - February 1958 in fact.

Of interest is that the Caernarfon to Dinas section of the route south from Bangor to Afonwen, near Pwllheli, is now the first part of the two-foot narrow gauge Welsh Highland Railway.

BELOW: *The 13.50 auto train from Leamington Spa Avenue to Coventry restarts from Kenilworth on 16th August 1958 behind push-pull fitted Ivatt 2MT 2-6-2T No. 41228.*

ABOVE: *'Jubilee' 4-6-0 No. 45637 'Windward Islands' and unrebuilt 'Royal Scot' 4-6-0 No. 46134 'The Cheshire Regiment' stand at the Euston bufferstops on 1st June 1951, following arrival with trains from Liverpool and Blackpool, respectively. No 45637 was scrapped following the Harrow & Wealdstone accident of 8th October 1952.*

BELOW: *Stanier 8F 2-8-0 No. 48122 departs from Euston on 3rd August 1958, with empty stock of the incoming 'Mancunian', at the same time as an Oerlikon EMU leaves for Watford Junction.*

ABOVE: *The inaugural service of 'The Shamrock' express for Liverpool Lime Street on 14th June 1954, due to depart from Euston at 16.55, is headed by Edge Hill (8A)-based Rebuilt 'Royal Scot' 4-6-0 No. 46153 'The Royal Dragoon'.*

BELOW: *An Oerlikon electric unit awaits departure from Euston to Watford Junction on 27th July 1957, alongside LMS 2P 4-4-0 No. 40683, which has arrived in the opposite platform with a service from Northampton.*

ABOVE: *Allocated to Crewe North shed (5A), unrebuilt 'Patriot' 4-6-0 No. 45546 'Fleetwood' is reversed on the Camden Town (1B) turntable on 6th July 1958, with the shed in the background containing 'Black 5' 4-6-0 No. 44942, 'Duchess' No. 46238 'City of Carlisle', rebuilt 'Patriot' No. 45528 and Caprotti 5MT 4-6-0 No. 44752.*

BELOW: *Stanier Class 8P Pacific No. 46200 'The Princess Royal' on the Cowans Sheldon 70ft vacuum-operated turntable at Camden Town on the same day. This locomotive was the last of the class withdrawn, in November 1962.*

ABOVE: *Fowler Class 3MT 2-6-2T No. 40070 heads empty coching stock from Euston to Wembley carriage sidings on 16th July 1958. Having topped Camden bank, the loco is heading down to the underpass leading to Primrose Hill tunnel.*

LEFT: *The 16.42 express working from Euston to Northampton and Stafford passes Camden Town shed (1B) later that afternoon with unrebuilt 'Patriot' 4-6-0 No. 45516 'The Hertfordshire and Bedfordshire Regiment' having slugged its way to the summit of Camden bank. The people outside the shed building are members of the Railway Photographic Society who were visiting at the time, and in view are Geoff Rixon, the late Maurice Early with the tripod and the late Lewis Coles who had arranged the trip. The locos that can be seen at the front of the building are 'Black 5' 4-6-0 No. 44752, 'Princess Coronation' Pacific No. 46238 'City of Carlisle' and rebuilt 'Patriot' No. 45528.*

Jubilee class 4-6-0 No. 45601 'British Guiana' powers up Camden Bank from Euston on 7th October 1958, with an express for Crewe, and passes BR Standard 4MT 2-6-4T No. 80068 hauling empty coaching stock for Camden Yard.

ABOVE: *Still retaining 'L M S' on the tender, unrebuilt 6P 'Royal Scot' 4-6-0 No. 46110 'Grenadier Guardsman' overfills its tender on Bushey troughs, as it heads north with an express for Llandudno and Holyhead on 19th May 1951.*

RIGHT: *A southbound fitted freight for Willesden passes Bushey on 25th March 1953, headed by Bowen-Cooke LNWR-designed Class G2a 7F 0-8-0 No. 48915.*

BELOW: *Stanier 'Black 5' 4-6-0 No. 44831 approaches Bushey troughs on 1st June 1951, powering an express from Llandudno to Euston.*

ABOVE: *Stanier 'Black 5' 4-6-0 No. 44751 fitted with Caprotti valve gear, pilots 'Jubilee' 4-6-0 No 45674 'Duncan' through Watford Junction on 9th August 1956, hauling a Euston–Manchester London Road express.*

BELOW: *Trundling through Stafford two days previously, on 7th August 1956, ex-L&NWR G2a 'Super D' 7F class 0-8-0 No. 49119 hauls a long mixed freight for Warrington.*

ABOVE: *'Black 5' 4-6-0 No. 44916 heads briskly away from Stafford, on 7th August 1958 with the 11.35 Blackpool-Birmingham train, unusually consisting of only three coaches. The impressive exhaust was more for the camera than the load!*

LEFT: *Carrying a Polmadie (66A) shedplate, Princess Coronation Class 8P Pacific No. 46232 'Duchess of Montrose' is on shed at Crewe North (5A) on 20th August 1956.*

ABOVE: *Threading a path through the seemingly multi-chimneyed Northwich station, Stanier 8F class 2-8-0 No. 48500 heads eastbound on 20th August 1955 with a train of ICI hoppers, while a Great Central 04 class 2-8-0 shunts the yard.*

LEFT: *Ex-Lancashire & Yorkshire Railway 0-6-0 No. 52341 awaits its next turn of duty at Wigan Springs Branch yards on 26th August 1955. Also in view are a Stanier 8F 2-8-0, Robinson ex-Great Central 'J10/6' 0-6-0 No. 65713 and Stanier 4MT 2-6-4T No. 42465.*

BELOW: *Passing Wigan Springs Branch on 26th August 1955, Stanier 'Black 5' 4-6-0 No. 44971, with a self-weighing tender, hauls a northbound freight for Carlisle.*

ABOVE: *Aspinall 1889-designed L&Y 2P 2-4-2T No. 50644 inside its home shed of Warrington (8B) on 23rd August 1955.*

BELOW: *Stanier 5MT Mogul No. 42949 of Brunswich (8E) shed awaits departure from Liverpool Central on 22nd August 1955, with the 11.43 local service to Stockport.*

ABOVE: *Complete with headboard, Princess Coronation 'Duchess' Pacific No. 46231 'Duchess of Atholl' hauls the southbound 'Mid-Day Scot' past Carlisle Upperby on 28th June 1957.*

BELOW: *Unrebuilt 'Patriot' 4-6-0 No. 45542 pulls away from Carlisle Upperby yards the same afternoon, with a southbound freight.*

ABOVE: *Stanier LMS 3MT 2-6-2T No. 40172 awaits departure from St Pancras on 3rd August 1958, with the empty coaching stock of a Sunday arrival at the terminus from Leicester.*

BELOW: *Hauling loaded hoppers to Wellingborough, Franco-Crosti boilered Class 9F 2-10-0 No. 92026 passes between Mill Hill Broadway and Elstree on 26th May 1957.*

ABOVE: *Hauling a six-coach suburban train of compartment stock near Mill Hill Broadway on 25th May 1957, BR Standard 4MT 4-6-0 No. 75041 has steam to spare with a local service from St Pancras to Bedford. The locomotive is attached to a BR2a-type inset tender.*

LEFT: *Fowler LMS-built Class 3MT 2-6-2T No. 40029 approaches Elstree tunnel on 21st March 1953, heading a local service from Luton (Midland Road) to St Pancras.*

BELOW: *Needing assistance with a 15-coach express from Nottingham to St Pancras on 25th May 1957, Class 5MT 'Black 5' 4-6-0 No. 45335 is piloted by Midland 2P class 4-4-0 No. 40485, and passes through Elstree & Borehamwood station. The 4-4-0 was one of the type with seven foot half-inch driving wheels that were introduced by Fowler from 1912 as rebuilds of original Johnson engines.*

ABOVE: *BR Standard 9F 2-10-0 No. 92026 heads south from Elstree Tunnel on 25th May 1957, hauling loaded coal wagons for Cricklewood.*

BELOW: *A local service from St Albans to St Pancras passes Silkstream Junction, Hendon, on 25th May 1957, headed by Fairburn 4MT class 2-6-4T No. 42178.*

ABOVE: *At Derby Midland station on 24th July 1955, Stanier 'Black 5' 4-6-0 No. 44981 of Bourneville shed (21B) awaits a clear signal with a southbound semi-fast service, while a Fowler 4MT 2-6-4T shunts empty stock in the adjacent platform.*

BELOW: *Johnson-designed Midland Railway 1F 0-6-0T No. 41699 outside Burton-on-Trent shed (17B) on 28th August 1955.*

ABOVE: *Fowler Class 2-6-4T No. 42407 at Wakefield Kirkgate on 27th August 1955, with a local train from Castleford. After the wellbeing of crews began to be taken into consideration, this was one of the batch built from 1933 with side-window cab and doors.*

BELOW: *Ivatt 4MT Mogul No. 43115 prepares to move the Leeds Holbeck breakdown train, which included a steam crane, away from 20A to answer a derailment call later on the same day.*

ABOVE: *Bournville (21B)-allocated Stanier 'Black 5' 4-6-0 No. 44981 nears Pontefract Baghill on 22nd May 1959, heading the 15.30 express from Newcastle to Birmingham New Street.*

BELOW: *Liverpool Bank Hall (27A) 'Black 5' 4-6-0 No. 45227 arrives at Blackburn on 25th August 1955, hauling an express from Liverpool Exchange.*

ABOVE: *A Fenchurch Street to Shoeburyness express service passes Bromley-by-Bow on 31st August 1957, hauled by Stanier three-cylinder 4MT 2-6-4T No. 42529, with a London Underground District Line train for Ealing Broadway in the other platform..*

BELOW: *Ex Johnson Midland Railway 1P 0-4-4T No. 58038 approaches Romford on 5th September 1952, propelling the 12.14 shuttle from Upminster.*

Eastern Region

Some of my favourite photographic locations were in this Region; the climb of Holloway Bank from King's Cross to Finsbury Park, the tunnels at Hadley Wood, Potters Bar and Welwyn, and the wonderful variety of motive power to be found passing through Doncaster, all available at lineside thanks to the most agreeable Eastern Region Public Relations staff.

On the line from Liverpool Street to East Anglia, I made frequent sorties to Brentwood Bank, where almost everything that passed by was going to Southend, Colchester, Ipswich, Norwich, Great Yarmouth or King's Lynn, and as a result there appeared no need at the time to travel further into Essex, Suffolk or Norfolk. An omission I now regret, but can do nothing about unless someone invents a real 'Tardis'! The route from London Marylebone was covered through the Chilterns, and the likes of Northwich, Gorton and Chester Northgate were also visited during the period.

As regards the variety of motive power, this was extensive and involved 140 different classes and sub classes with external differences, many of which could be found on the Eastern and North Eastern Regions, into which the old LNER was split, and across the Border in Scotland. Unlike the Midland Region, classes were easy to identify, as letters of the alphabet coincided with the wheel arrangements, i.e. all the Pacifics started with 'A', the 4-6-0s with 'B', the Atlantics with 'C', and so on to the 0-4-2s, which began with a 'Z'. I failed to catch up with just three of the many types before they were withdrawn, the Great Northern 'J2' 0-6-0, the Manchester, Sheffield & Lincolnshire Railway 'N4' 0-6-2Ts and the Beyer-Garratt class U1.

ABOVE:
Rebuilt in 1937 from Gresley's experimental high-pressure four-cylinder compound, the sole Class W 4-6-4 No. 60700 rests inside its home shed of Doncaster (36A) on 31st August 1954.

ABOVE: *A relief for the 'Aberdonian' at King's Cross on 11th January 1952, with Class A3 Pacific No. 60112 'St Simon' simmering in the platform. The 'Aberdonian' itself was not due into the Granite City until breakfast time; this portion probably arrived in time for lunch!*

BELOW: *The 12.18 Sunday express from King's Cross to Newcastle passes under the North London Line viaduct that spans the East Coast Main LIne at Belle Isle, between Gasworks and Copenhagen tunnels, on 13th July 1952, powered by A3 class Pacific No. 60056 'Centenary', this view taken from Belle Isle signalbox steps.*

ABOVE: *Making an impressive sight emerging from Copenhagen Tunnel and beginning the climb of Holloway Bank, Class A3 Pacific No. 60063 'Isinglass' works a King's Cross to Peterborough semi-fast service on 8th May 1955.*

RIGHT: *'The Norseman', the 09.00 boat train from King's Cross to Newcastle Tyne Commission Quay, bursts from Copenhagen Tunnel on 11th July 1953, powered by Gresley Class V2 2-6-2 No. 60966 of Peterborough New England shed (35A).*

BELOW: *A4 class Pacific No. 60034 'Lord Faringdon' climbs away from Copenhagen Tunnel and commences the climb to Holloway summit on 11th May 1954, powering the 17.30 King's Cross-Harrogate 'Yorkshire Pullman'..*

THE
NORSEMAN
60966
35A

ABOVE: *'A4s' on freight were never a common sight, and when one did turn up, always looked incongruous. Before the station was renamed Alexandra Palace, No. 60010 'Dominion of Canada' passes Wood Green on 19th September 1952, hauling fish vans from Aberdeen, most of the contents of which will eventually arrivee at Billingsgate Market.*

BELOW: *Gangers stand aside as Class B1 4-6-0 No. 61027 'Madoqua' emerges from Hadley North tunnel with a mixed freight from Peterborough to King's Cross goods on 13th July 1952.*

ABOVE: *'One of the large fleet of Gresley N2/2 class 0-6-2Ts allocated to King's Cross shed (34A) for local services, No. 69506 restarts from the Hadley Wood stop on 1st July 1952, heading the 19.21 from King's Cross to Welwyn Garden City. .*

BELOW: *A rare locomotive type to be seen on the Great Northern main line, Holden-designed ex-Great Eastern Railway 'Claud Hamilton' D16/3 class 4-4-0 No. 62618 emerges from Hadley North tunnel on 19th July 1952, working a Cambridge-King's Cross semi-fast train. Rebuilt from a Belpaire-boilered Class D16/2, the engine still retains its original decorative valencing and was once the 'Royal Engine'.*

ABOVE: *On the chill morning of 28th September 1952, the weak sunshine helps clear away both mist and frost as Class A4 Pacific No. 60007 'Sir Nigel Gresley' pounds up the 1 in 200 gradient towards Potters Bar with the 09.15 'Centenaries Express' special from King's Cross to York. Consisting mainly of Gresley wooden-bodied coaching stock, the train was run to commemorate, among other things, the opening of King's Cross station 100 years earlier..*

BELOW: *With Potters Bar cutting increased to four tracks, but prior to the new tunnel bores at Hadley Wood and Potters Bar being completed to allow the new four-track section to extend further south, Gresley B17/4 class 4-6-0 No. 61652 'Darlington' approaches Potters Bar station on 16th July 1955, heading a northbound 'Cambridge Buffet Express'.*

ABOVE: *Having crossed Welwyn Viaduct, ex-War Department 2-8-0 No. 90158 passes through Welwyn North station on 17th April 1954, hauling a long mixed freight from Hornsey yards to Grantham.*

BELOW: *Inside the busy repair shops of New England (35A) shed on 24th May 1959, attention is given to a variety of engines, including Class A5/1 Pacific tank No. 69827, Class A4 Pacific No. 60008 'Dwight D. Eisenhower' and Class A3 Pacific No. 60082 'Neil Gow'.*

ABOVE: *During its days fitted with a double chimney, A3 class Pacific No. 60103 'Flying Scotsman' awaits its next duty on shed at Doncaster (36A) on 23rd May 1959.*

BELOW: *A Newcastle-King's Cross express accelerates away from the Doncaster stop on 31st August 1954, powered by Class V2 2-6-2 No. 60982.*

ABOVE: *Making an attempt to black-out Doncaster, Class B17/1 'Sandringham' 4-6-0 No. 61643 'Champion Lodge' departs from the station on 31st August 1954, with the 09.07 semi-fast train for Peterborough.*

BELOW: *A Robinson design for the Great Central Railway, Class J11 0-6-0 No. 64404 trundles into Doncaster from the north on 31st August 1954, hauling a Sheffield-bound freight working.*

ABOVE: *The last of Stirling's Hull & Barnsley Railway 0-6-2Ts, Class N3 No. 69114, inside Leeds Neville Hill (50B) shed just prior to withdrawal on 26th August 1955.*

BELOW: *Frodingham (36C)-based Robinson Great Central 04/1 class 2-8-0 No. 63601 passes Trent Junction, near Scunthorpe, on 23rd May 1959 with a freight for Doncaster. Today this locomotive is in the care of the National Railway Museum and appropriately, is based on the Great Central Railway at Loughborough.*

ABOVE: *The inaugural 'Starlight Special' to Glasgow St Enoch awaits departure from Marylebone on 10th April 1953, behind Neasden (34E)-allocated 'A3' Pacific No. 60111 'Enterprise'.*

BELOW: *Thompson Class L1 2-6-4T No. 67781 steams downgrade between Beaconsfield and Seer Green on 8th July 1952, heading the 08.16 service from High Wycombe to Marylebone. The distinctive clanking sound of the motion on these rough-riding engines resulted in them being nicknamed 'cement mixers'.*

ABOVE: *It was the custom for part of the 1950s for Alan Pegler to charter a special train for his Northern Rubber Company employees to have a day out. He usually found unusual motive power for the chosen route, and on 6th June 1953 it was D11/1 class 4-4-0 No. 62666 Zeebrugge' that was in use when the train traversed the route through the Chilterns, seen here approaching High Wycombe.*

BELOW: *Class D11/1 4-4-0 No 62664 'Princess Mary' pilots Ivatt 2MT 2-6-2T No. 41215 on a Manchester Exchange-Chester Northgate semi-fast service on 20th August 1955, approaching Northwich.*

ABOVE: *Class D11/1 'Director' 4-4-0 No. 62661 'Gerard Powys Dewhurst' has its tender raked over at Chester Northgate prior to leaving with a service for Manchester Central*

LEFT: *A visit to Gorton Works and shed on 24th August 1955 revealed Robinson Great Central D11/1 4-4-0 No. 62662 'Prince of Wales' undergoing a heavy overhaul.*

BELOW: *Robinson Great Central 1903-designed C13 class 4-4-2T No. 67401 coaled and watered and ready to go at Gorton shed (39A) the same morning.*

LEFT: *It used to be a tradition for the Liverpool Street station pilot to receive a distinctive livery, unlike any other locomotive of the Stratford (30A) allocation. In the early 1950s, the role was given to this Class J69/1 0-6-0T, which was put into green and given its first BR number of E8619. On 22nd August 1951, the immaculate 0-6-0T was engaged in shunting wagons on one of the non-platform roads.*

BELOW LEFT: *Liverpool Street station is very different today to what it was when this scene was taken on 11th May 1951. With rays of spring sunshine manfully endeavouring to penetrate the sulphurous interior, Class N7/2 0-6-2T No. 69681 awaits departure with a local service for Hertford East.*

BELOW: *'The East Anglian' express for Norwich awaits departure time at Liverpool Street on 11th March 1952, headed by one of the Stratford (30A) 'Britannia 'Pacifics No. 70002 'Geoffrey Chaucer'.*

ABOVE: *In days when Bethnal Green station sported quite ornate platform canopies and some of Stratford shed's loco allocation received smokebox embellishments, Class N7/5 0-6-2T No. 69669 makes the prescribed stop with the 18.07 local service from Liverpool Street to Enfield Town.*

LEFT: *With steam seemingly exuding from every orifice, Class N7/2 0-6-2T No. 69694 restarts from Crouch End on 10th April 1954, with the 16.02 'Ally Pally' auto service from Finsbury Park to Alexandra Palace.*

BELOW: *With a local service for Hertford East departing from the Bethnal Green platform on the left, tender-first K3/2 class Mogul No. 61810 passes on the through line in the opposite direction, hauling empty coaching stock for London Liverpool Street.*

ABOVE: *Holden Great Eastern Class F5 2-4-2T No. 67219 receives the signal to depart from Stratford (Low Level) station on 8th August 1953, with the 12.45 local service from North Woolwich to Palace Gates.*

BELOW: *Having been derailed following a collision outside Stratford 'New Shed' on 5th September 1953, Class J69/2 0-6-0T No. 68510 is crane-lifted back onto the tracks. Damage was minimal and the loco remained in service at Stratford Depot (30A) until 1959.*

ABOVE: *The one and only K5 class Mogul was allocated to Stratford, from where it was photographed on 23rd April 1955. No. 61863 retained its number when rebuilt in 1945 by Thompson as a two-cylinder version of a Gresley three-cylinder Class K3. It appeared not to be very popular for use at Stratford, as it could usually be found in this way on shed out of use.*

BELOW: *Considering their 0-4-0 wheel arrangement, the five Hill-designed Great Eastern Class Y4 dock tanks were quite powerful engines. Constructed at Stratford in 1913, they worked in the East London area throughout their existence, and four were finally withdrawn between 1955 and 1957, the one remaining being Departmental Stock No 33, which survived until closure of Stratford old works in 1963. On 19th March 1956, No. 68128 waits to haul loaded trucks away from one of Stratford Shed's coal lines, after being loaded by crane. This area contained a huge stockpile of coal that served the five different sheds that made up the Stratford complex.*

ABOVE: *Some 68-years-old and still going strong. Worsdell's 1886 designed Great Eastern J15 class 0-6-0 No. 65370 departs from Temple Mills yards on 10th April 1954, with a loose-coupled freight for Colchester.*

LEFT: *A K3 Mogul was uncommon motive power for Liverpool Street-Southend-on-Sea passenger traffic, but nevertheless No. 61835 was brought into use for such a working on 9th May 1953, and is shown here pounding up the 1-in-85 of Brentwood Bank towards Ingrave summit.*

BELOW: *Passing east of Shenfield, where the electrification then ended, 'BR 'Britannia' Pacific No. 70003 'John Bunyan' hauls a Liverpool Street-Norwich express on 10th May 1952.*

ABOVE: *Ivatt 2MT class Mogul No. 46402 departs from Cambridge on 8th August 1953, with the 11.27 train for Huntingdon and Kettering. In the mainline platform, Class D16/3 4-4-0 No. 62606 waits to leave, heading the 11.33 service from March.*

BELOW: *Ivatt Class 2MT Mogul No. 46467 brakes for the scheduled stop at Bartlow on 27th April 1958, hauling the 16.02 local service from Cambridge to Marks Tey.*

North Eastern Region

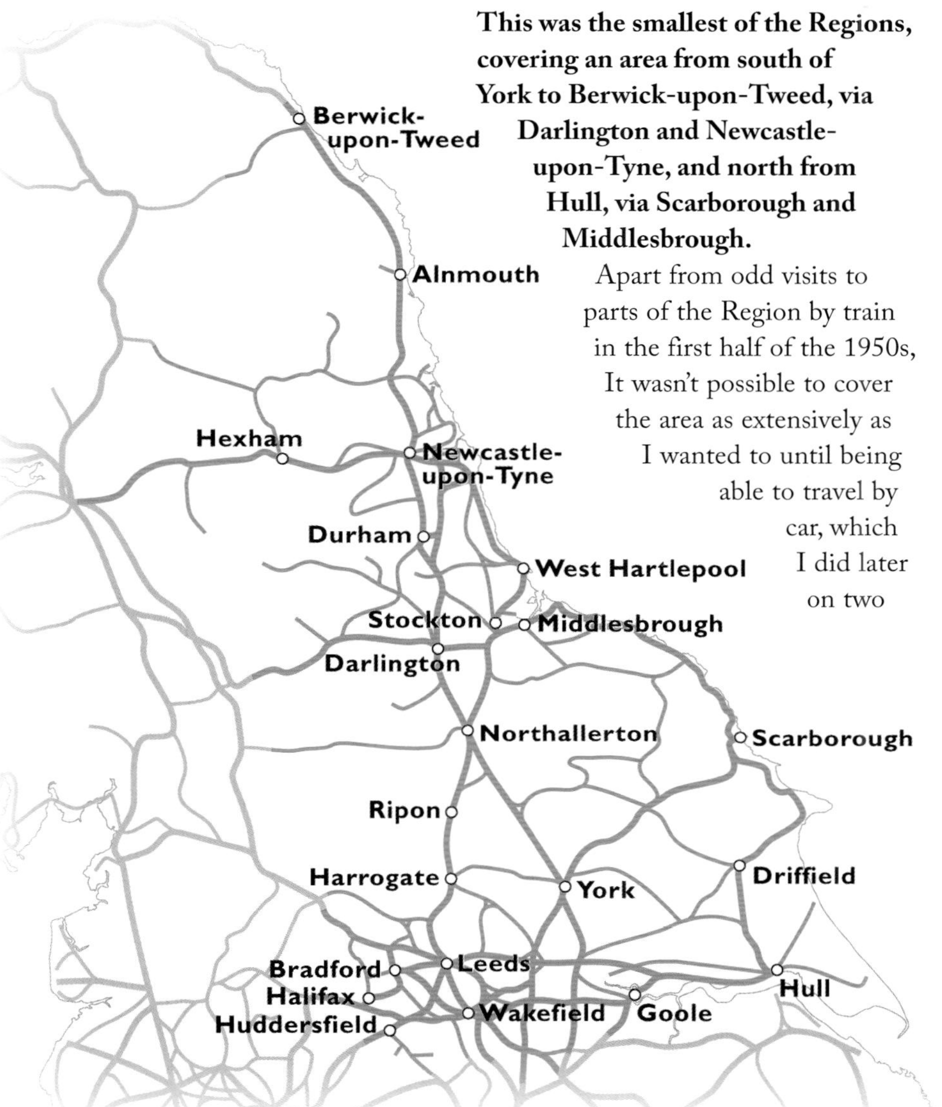

This was the smallest of the Regions, covering an area from south of York to Berwick-upon-Tweed, via Darlington and Newcastle-upon-Tyne, and north from Hull, via Scarborough and Middlesbrough.

Apart from odd visits to parts of the Region by train in the first half of the 1950s, It wasn't possible to cover the area as extensively as I wanted to until being able to travel by car, which I did later on two occasions, each trip lasting for a week.

My application for a lineside photographic pass was acted upon by return of post – and it was my first all-Region one. This enabled visits for the first time to some of the more difficult sheds locations, such as Tyne Dock, Heaton and Thornaby, but I still didn't manage to include the routes from Newcastle to Berwick or Newcastle to Carlisle, via Hexham.

Having been part of the LNER before Nationalisation in 1948, much of the variety of motive power was shared with Eastern Region, but there were some types that rarely if ever travelled south, such as the A7s, A8s, G5s, J25s, J26s, J27s, J77s, J88s, N8s, N9s, N10s, N13s, N14s, N15s, Q1s, Q6s, Q7s, S1s and T1s.

BELOW: *Passing Heaton with empty mineral hoppers, Raven-designed 1921-introduced superheated Class J27 0-6-0 No 65877 heads northwards on 27th August 1954. Only one of this type of locomotive survived in to preservation, in the form of No. 65894. The locomotive, owned by the North Eastern Locomotive Preservation Group, is currently out of boiler certificate.*

60072

LEFT: *The sole Class A1/1 Pacific No 60113 'Great Northern' makes the scheduled stop at Yprk on 29th August 1954, heading an exprss from King's Cross to Newcastle. The loco was a Thompson rebuild of a Gresley A10 Pacific, that was then developed by Peppercorn as the eventual new A1 class.*

BELOW LEFT: *Curving away from the stop at York on 21st May 1959, 'A3' Pacific No 60072 'Sunstar' hauls a Bristol Temple Meads-Newcastle cross-country express. The locomotive was one of just two that were allocated to Tweedmouth shed (52D) at the time.*

BELOW: *Departing from York on 21st May 1959, 'Jubilee' 4-6-0 No 45719 'Glorious' heads a Scarborough-Liverpool Exchange express, while Class 3F 'Jinty' 0-6-0T No 47556 shunts empty coaching stock in the adjacent platform. Class B16/2 4-6-0 No 61421 awaits a clear signal to proceed 'light engine' to York South shed.*

ABOVE: *Avoiding York station by way of Skelton and Holgate Junctions, BR Standard 9F 2-10-9 No. 92177 heads south past Holgate sidings on 22nd May 1959.*

LEFT: *Fitted with a double chimney, 'A3' Pacific No. 60050 'Persimmon' departs from York on the same morning, hauling an express from Newcastle to King's Cross. The roundhouse is York South shed, a subsidiary to York (50A) and not given a shed code of its own.*

BELOW: *Passing York shed and locos coaling up, including 'Black 5' 4-6-0 No. 45269 and 8F 2-8-0 No. 48150, Class 3F 'Jinty' 0-6-0T No. 47334 is engaged in shunting a Gresley Brake Third coach later the same day.*

ABOVE: *Selby (50C) resident Class D20/1 4-4-0 No. 62374 on its home shed on 30th August 1954. The loco was an 1889 Worsdell design for the North Eastern Railway.*

BELOW: *A westbound freight working for Hull Dairycoates rounds the curve at Selby on 22nd May 1959, hauled by Gresley K3/2 class Mogul No. 61902.*

ABOVE: *A Hull to Liverpool Central express near Selby on 23rd May 1959 is worked by Selby (50C)-based Thompson B1 class 4-6-0 No. 61237 'Geoffrey H. Kitson'.*

ABOVE RIGHT: *A Newcastle to King's Cross express passes non-stop through Selby on 22nd May 1959, powered by A4 class Pacific No. 60017 'Silver Fox'.*

BELOW: *The King's Cross-bound 'Talisman' express from Edinburgh Waverley on 22nd May 1959, recovers from the 25mph speed restriction through Selby, and 'A2' Pacific No. 60539 'Bronzino' pulls away round the curve under clear signals. The locomotive was to last just another three years, being one of the first three 'A2s' to be withdrawn in November 1962.*

ABOVE: *Introduced by Worsdell for the North Eastern Railway in 1909, York (50A)-allocated T1 class 0-8-4T No. 69910 stands at Selby shed on 23rd May 1959, awaiting boiler replenishment.*

BELOW: *Leeds Neville Hill (50B)-based 'A3' Pacific No. 60084 'Trigo' pulls away from Harrogate on 22nd May 1959, with the 'Queen of Scots' Pullman, bound for London King's Cross.*

ABOVE: *Passing Ripon Line Junction, south of Thirsk, on 21st May 1959, B1 class 4-6-0 No 61220 heads north with empty steel-carrying wagons. In addition to the engine driver, an unknown gentleman in a suit and trilby hat looks out of the cab!*

BELOW: *Not travelling at 126mph but still passing near Thirsk at a fair turn of speed, 'A4' Pacific world-speed record holder No 60022 'Mallard' heads the northbound 'Flying Scotsman' on the same day.*

ABOVE: *Raven-designed NER Class B16/1 4-6-0 No. 61473 heads through Thirsk on 21st May 1959, hauling a southbound freight for York.*

LEFT: *Powering a Newcastle-Colchester cross-country express, Gresley V2 class 2-6-2 No. 60812 passes through Thirsk station at speed on on the same day.*

BELOW: *Later that afternoon, an unusual locomotive combination running south of Thirsk was WD class 2-8-0 No. 90027 piloting Blackstone-engined Class 10 diesel shunter No 13141 on a southbound mixed freight. The shunter was probably part of the consist being taken to or from works.*

ABOVE: *Approaching the Stockton & Darlington Railway crossing at Darlington with clear signals, Class B1 4-6-0 No. 61062 heads north with an express working on 28th August 1954.*

BELOW: *With mailbags and a young spotter draped on the opposite platform, Blaydon (52C)-allocated D49/2 class 4-4-0 No. 62771 'The Rufford' departs from Newcastle Central on 27th August 1954, heading the 17.10 semi-fast train for Saltburn.*

ABOVE: *Class A8 Pacific tank No. 69891 departs from Darlington Bank Top on 28th August 1954, hauling a stopping service for Saltburn. These engines were a Gresley rebuild of the 1913 Raven-designed fleet of 4-4-4Ts.*

BELOW: *The 16.35 Inter-Regional express from Newcastle to Oxford leaves Darlington Bank Top on the same day behind V2 class 2-6-2 No 60934. On the left, Class A8 Pacific tank No. 69859 heads the 17.56 service for Saltburn.*

ABOVE: *Restarting from a signal check at Darlington, the regular heavy train of fish vans from Aberdeen to King's Cross is hauled by Class A2/3 Pacific No. 60512 'Steady Aim' on 20th May 1959.*

BELOW: *Class Q6 0-8-0 No. 63375 hauls hoppers southwards at Thornaby on 28th August 1954, and passes Class J94 0-6-0ST No. 68037 awaiting exit from the yards.*

ABOVE: *Northbound coke hoppers pass Stranton Crossing, near West Hartlepool, on 20th May 1959, hauled by Raven-designed North Eastern Railway Q6 class 0-8-0 No 63391.*

BELOW: *Designed by William Worsdell for the NER in 1898, Class J25 0-6-0 No (6)5658 is in use as a stationary boiler at Gateshead shed (52A) on 26th August 1954 - accompanied a wheelbarrow!*

ABOVE: *North Eastern Railway Class J72 0-6-0T No. 68702 is watered up by the crew in the yard at Heaton shed (52B) on 27th August 1954.*

BELOW: *Having arrived at Newcastle behind Class A1 Pacific No .60159 'Bonnie Dundee', motive power is changed on the southbound 'Heart of Midlothian' and 'A4' No 60016 'Silver King' takes over earlier that day.*

ABOVE: *Exclusively a freight shed, the locomotive allocation of Tyne Dock (54B) in the middle 1950s consisted mainly of Class Q6 and Q7 0-8-0s, J25 and J72 0-6-0s and the odd T1 4-8-0T, N9 0-6-2T and WD 2-8-0s. Specially placed for the camera outside the depot on 26th August 1954, is 'Q7' No 63462 wth its cheerful crew posing in the cab. .*

BELOW: *Also present was J25 class 0-6-0 No. 65694 pictured in the roundhouse, awaiting its next duty*

ABOVE: *One of the last three NER N9 0-6-2Ts to remain in service on 26th August 1954 was No 69427, all three locomotives finishing their days allocated to Tyne Dock shed (54B), where this photo was taken.*

BELOW: *One of Worsdell's large NER Class T1 4-8-0Ts No 69921 is watered up in the yards at Tyne Dock shed (54B) on 28th August 1954.*

Scottish Region

My ancestry comes from a fairly long line of lighthouse keepers on the Isle of Skye, and holiday visits north of the Border were made on a number of occasions in the 1950s to visit relations, principally in Aberdeen.

Scottish Region kindly issued me an all-Region lineside permit, which allowed the other Scottish cities to be covered, all by train travel, although I failed to get to some of the more difficult coastal venues such as Stranraer, Oban, Mallaig, Wick, Thurso and Fraserburgh. My one trip to Kyle of Lochalsh and back took a whole day, and, as stated in the caption, resulted in one photograph being taken in pouring rain! Generally, however, the weather is kind to me in Scotland and plenty of sunshine is apparent on the various exposures taken in Dumfries, Edinburgh, Dunfermline, Glasgow, Greenock, Kilmarnock, Stirling, Perth, Dundee, Aberdeen, Aviemore and Inverness.

A lot of the motive power north of the Border is exclusive to the Region, but much of it was also shared with the Eastern, Midland and North Eastern Regions, a legacy from the days when Scotland was part of both the LMS and the LNER. Classes C15, C16, D20, D30, D40, J35, J36, J37, J83, V1, V3, V4, Y9, Z4 and Z5s were all exclusive to Scotland, and were designed for the Region or were taken on by the LNER from their origins on the Great North of Scotland and North British Railways, and I am pleased to say that I succeeded in satisfactorily recording examples of all of them on film.

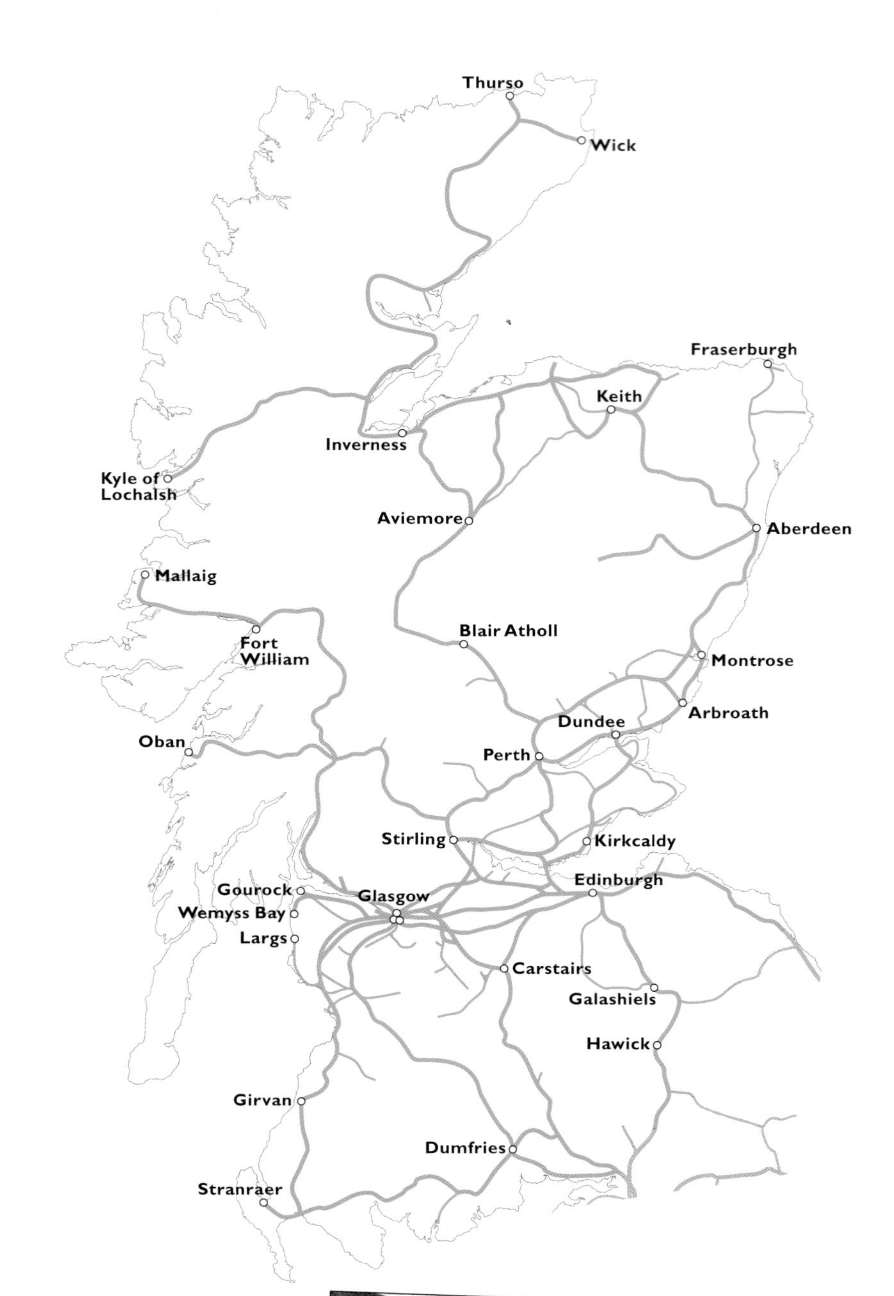

RIGHT: *Chalked 'Tank Empty' and 'Boiler Empty', Manning Wardle Great North of Scotland Railway Class Z5 0-4-2 Dock Tank No 68192 stands outside Kittybrewster shed (61A) on 25th June 1957.*

ABOVE: *Class 2P 4-4-0 No 40616 stands at Dumfries on 29th June 1957, after arrival with the 10.58 train from Stranraer.*

BELOW: *Hauling along mixed freight from Carlisle Kingmoor, Jubilee class 4-6-0 No 45732 'Sanspareil' heads north through Dumfries later that morning.*

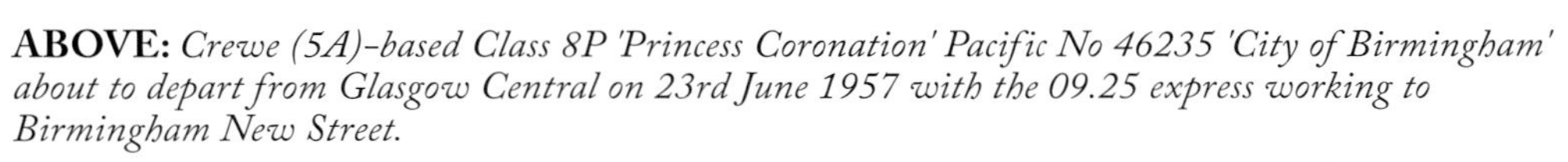
ABOVE: *Crewe (5A)-based Class 8P 'Princess Coronation' Pacific No 46235 'City of Birmingham' about to depart from Glasgow Central on 23rd June 1957 with the 09.25 express working to Birmingham New Street.*

BELOW: *Leeds Holbeck (55A)-allocated Royal Scot' 4-6-0 No 46117 'Welsh Guardsman' awaits departure from Glasgow St Enoch on 29th June 1957, with the 'Starlight Special' for London Marylebone.*

ABOVE: *Caledonian 2F 'Jumbo' 0-6-0 No 57239, having just 'coaled up' at Glasgow Polmadie (66A) shed on 23rd June 1957.*

BELOW: *When taking this photograph at Glasgow Eastfield shed (65A) on 23rd June 1957, I had no idea that I would still be able to see Gresley K4 class Mogul No 61994 'The Great Marquess' working on the main line over 50 years later - and on the West Highland lines for which it was designed by Gresley in 1937!*

ABOVE: *Longmore Military Railway 2-10-0 No. 601 'Kitchener' was an unexpected visitor to Glasgow Eastfield shed (65A) on 23rd June 1957, the immaculate blue-liveried locomotive standing with J50/3 class 0-6-0T No 68950 and 'C16' 4-4-2T No 67485.*

ABOVE: *Caledonian 2F class 'Jumbo' 0-6-0 No 57364 under major overhaul in St Rollox Works on 23rd June 1957, accompanied by No 57446 of the same class and 'Jubilee' 4-6-0 No 45721 'Sanspareil'.*

BELOW: *BR Standard 5MT 4-6-0 No 73148, fitted with Caprotti valve gear, on the turntable at St Rollox shed (65B) the same day.*

ABOVE: *A Gresley predecessor to the more prolific J39 class, J38 0-6-0 No 65905 undergoes a heavy overhaul in Cowlairs Works on 23rd June 1957.*

BELOW: *Also present for overhaul was Reid-designed North British Railway Class J88 0-6-0 No 68354 from Polmont shed (64E)*

ABOVE: *Passing the magnificent array of semaphore signals controlled by Greenock Princes Pier signalbox, Pickersgill-designed Caledonian Railway '928' class 3P 4-4-0 No 54468 marshalls empty coaching stock to form a train from Princes Pier station for Glasgow St Enoch on 22nd June 1957.*

RIGHT: *Coming under the same fine 17-arm signal gantry approaching Greenock Princes Pier, Fairburn 4MT 2-6-4T No 42247 heads the 12.40 service from Glasgow St Enoch on that afternoon.*

BELOW: *Towards the middle of that afternoon, Fairburn 4MT 2-6-4T No 42190 awaits departure from Greenock Princes Pier station with the 14.20 Saturday train to Glasgow St Enoch.*

ABOVE: *Permanently attached to a somewhat makeshift wooden tender, Holmes-designed North British 1882-built Class Y9 0-4-0ST No. 68117 stands on shed at Kipps (65E) on 22nd June 1957.*

BELOW: *Later the same day, locos on shed at Greenock Ladyburn (66D) included Caledonian 0F 0-4-0ST No. 56031 and Caledonian 439 class 2P 0-4-4T No. 55267, both residents.*

ABOVE: *In exemplary condition, two ex-LMS Class 2P 4-4-0s from Hurlford (67B) and Ayr (67C) sheds, respectively, await departure from Kilmarnock on 29th June 1957. No. 40612 heads the 15.38 to Ardrossan (Winton Pier) and No. 40610 has the 16.00 train to Heads of Ayr.*

BELOW: *A grubby 'Royal Scot' 4-6-0 No. 46113 'Cameronian' approaches Kilmarnock on the same afternoon with the 15.50 Saturday express from Glasgow St Enoch to Dumfries.*

ABOVE: *'The Elizabethan' for London King's Cross departs from Edinburgh Waverley on 25th June 1953, with motive power provided by Haymarket (64B)-based Class A4 Pacific No. 60004 'William Whitelaw'.*

BELOW: *Arriving at Edinburgh Waverley with a local service from North Berwick on the same day, North British Railway 'Glen' class D34 4-4-0 No. 62490 'Glen Fintaig' is made to look fairly insignificant beneath one of the Edinburgh castle ramparts.*

ABOVE: *A 1927 Robinson design for the Great Central Railway, D49 class 4-4-0 No. 62692 'Allan-Bane' stands on shed at Haymarket (64B) on 26th June 1957.*

BELOW: *J37 class 0-6-0 No. 64565 approaches Dunfermline on 1st August 1953, hauling a northbound summer special.*

ABOVE: *With its only classmate No. 61700 being named 'Bantam Cock', it was probably inevitable that No. 61701, although not named, should be known as 'Bantam Hen'. On 24th June 1957, it heads the 06.25 'trip' freight from Aberdeen Yard to Laurencekirk. Class J39/3 0-6-0 No. 64975 is alongside.*

LEFT: *Three of an original fleet of six Class N14 0-6-2Ts built for the North British in 1909 survived to be taken into BR stock in 1948, and No. 69125 was the very last in service, being withdrawn soon after this view of it as it passes through Aberdeen on 29th July 1953, with a rake of empty coaching stock.*

BELOW: *Aberdeen Corporation Gas Department 0-4-0ST, believed to be No. 3 built by Andrew Barclay Sons & Co, Kilmarnock, in 1926, pulls away from Waterloo Quay on the Aberdeen Harbour Line on 26th June 1957, hauling tank wagons.*

ABOVE: *The 09.25 Elgin-Aberdeen train, via Buckie and Portsoy, and the 09.30 between the same two stations,but via Craigellachie and Keith, join at the exchange station known as Cairnie Junction on 25th June 1957. B1 class 4-6-0 No. 61324 has come off the 09.30 portion and all six coaches will now be taken onto their destination by Kittybrewster (61A)-allocated No. 61343 of the same class.*

BELOW: *Approaching Inverurie on 25th June 1957, Thompson B1 class 4-6-0 No. 61400 heads the 12.20 three-coach local service from Keith to Aberdeen..*

ABOVE: *The 10.52 service to Keith awaits departure from Forres on 29th July 1953, behind ex-Caledonian 920 class 3P 4-4-0 No. 54471.*

BELOW: *Great North of Scotland Railway Class D40 4-4-0 No. 62264 on shed at Keith (61C) on 28th July 1953.*

ABOVE: *Passing through Perth at dawn on 24th June 1957, WD 2-8-0 No. 90705 heads for Dunfermline with a mixture of wooden-bodied and steel-sided coal wagons.*

BELOW: *With the train on which I was travelling from Perth to Inverness halted on the left, there was time to make a hasty exit and photograph 'Black 5' 4-6-0 No. 45125 shunting in the yard at Blair Atholl on 24th June 1957.*

ABOVE: *Class 5MT 'Black 5' 4-6-0s Nos. 45459 and 45165 restart the 09.25 Edinburgh Princes Street–Inverness express from the stop at Aviemore on 24th June 1957.*

BELOW: *The 17.15 sleeping car train from Inverness to London Euston nears Culloden Moor on 27th July 1953, powered by double-headed 'Black 5' 4-6-0s Nos. 44979 and 44698.*

LEFT: *Drummond Highland Railway 'Small Ben' 2P 4-4-0 No. 54398 'Ben Alder' was one of 20 of the class built just before the turn of the century and was one of only three to receive a British Railways number in 1948. On 26th July 1953, it was a surprise 'find' in the Cairngorm Works yard in Inverness as it had been withdawn months earlier. I later learnt that it was scheduled for preservation, but was in fact broken up, some say by accident, others by design.*

BELOW: *Drummond Highland Railway 1P 0-4-4T No. 55053 undergoes repair inside Lochgorm Works, Inverness, on 24th June 1957. The last examples of the Highland Railway to remain in service, the two engines of the class were retained to work the branch line from Dornoch to The Mound. Both were withdrawn in the year that this scene was recorded.*

ABOVE: *The 09.15 train for Tain awaits departure from Inverness on 27th July 1953, headed by 'Black 5' 4-6-0 No. 44979.*

BELOW: *Shot of the day - the ONLY shot of the day! Train travel from Inverness in the 1950s was not particularly speedy and a return ticket to have a look at Kyle of Lochalsh on 28th July 1953 was met at the terminus by pouring rain. With the Isle of Skye shrouded in mist, Caledonian Railway 439 class 2P 0-4-4T No. 55316 shunts the yard next to the station's island platform.*